Mindful
Gardening

Mindful Gardening

find peace and calm in your outdoor space

CICO BOOKS

LONDON NEW YORK

Published in 2023 by CICO Books
An imprint of Ryland Peters & Small Ltd
20–21 Jockey's Fields   341 E 116th St
London WC1R 4BW   New York, NY 10029

www.rylandpeters.com

10 9 8 7 6 5 4 3 2 1

A CIP catalog record for this book is available from the Library
of Congress and the British Library.

ISBN: 978-1-80065-198-2

Printed in China

Designer: Louise Leffler
Commissioning editor: Kristine Pidkameny
Art director: Sally Powell
Creative director: Leslie Harrington
Head of production: Patricia Harrington
Publishing manager: Penny Craig

Contents

introduction

In both life and nature, there is profound wisdom. Be inspired by this collection of beautiful words and images about the magic of mindfulness in tending an outdoor space. When you devote time and energy to growing plants, vegetables, and flowers, it is richly rewarding; in doing so, you care for nature and the planet, as well as create a beautiful and sustaining space. This book celebrates the joy of doing just that, with a carefully curated selection of quotes and inspirational photography, as well as advice and simple suggestions on nurturing your own outdoor space, no matter how big or small.

The three sections in this book are an invitation to care, create and connect in your garden with a mindful approach. Mindfulness is deliberately paying attention to things we normally would not even notice, and becoming aware of our present moment experience as it arises, non-judgmentally, and with kindness and compassion. We use our senses—sight, sound, taste, touch, and smell—to explore our experience and activate the calming response. What better setting for this than the garden?

Your outdoor space is truly a gift. It is an opportunity to grow your own delights, as well as nurture and broaden your perspective about gratitude, community, and the natural rhythms of daily living. Inspired by the amazing colors and textures that nature offers cultivates curiosity to create some beauty of your own, perhaps even let your garden go wild. There are many ways to enrich your connection to nature through gardening and mindfulness. Within these pages, you'll find evocative images and guiding words to discover the stillness of quiet, the power of calm, and the joy of home-grown harvest and harmony.

Nature does not hurry, yet
everything is accomplished.

Lao Tzu

1

Caring

for Nature
and the Planet

Life begins the day you start a garden.

Chinese Proverb

Expanding Our Horizons

Apart from the physical exercise of gardening, being outside instantly expands our perspective and encourages us to look outward rather than stay stuck in internal overthinking.

There is much to learn from nature. However freezing and gray winter is, the day will come when we notice a bud breaking, feel the warmth of the wind rather than its chill, and realize that the weather has shifted. The natural world reminds us that everything passes at some point.

Being outdoors is a sensory rollercoaster that can place us right in the present moment: the damp potting compost running through our fingers, the sharp tang of a freshly torn basil leaf, the sweetness of a picked strawberry, the sighing of the wind through the trees…

Gardening is an opportunity to nurture—to plant a seed, care for it as it sprouts, support it as it grows tall, and appreciate its beauty or bounty. We can benefit from gardening, whether or not we have a garden. Wherever you live, there is always room for a pot on a windowsill. Planting seeds is a great opportunity to grow your mindfulness.

The real voyage of
discovery consists not in
seeking new landscapes,
but in having new eyes.

MARCEL PROUST

At the moment of commitment the entire Universe conspires to assist you.

JOHANN WOLFGANG VON GOETHE

A light wind swept over the corn,
and all nature laughed in the sunshine.

ANNE BRONTË

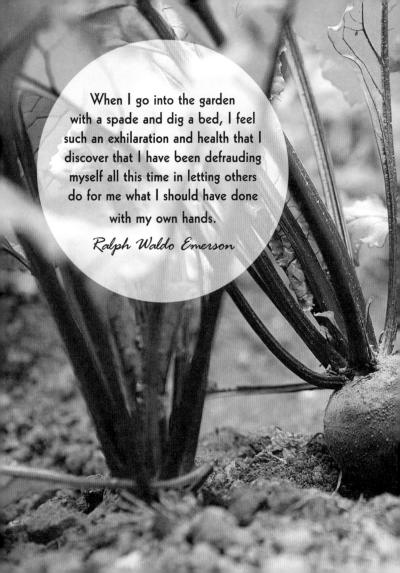

When I go into the garden
with a spade and dig a bed, I feel
such an exhilaration and health that I
discover that I have been defrauding
myself all this time in letting others
do for me what I should have done
with my own hands.

Ralph Waldo Emerson

Garden as though you will live forever.

WILLIAM KENT

Sunrise

Noonday sun

Sunset

The cycle of life

Listen and Breathe

Think of nature as a friend, a person
to spend time with in your garden.
Open your heart just as you would to
another human being. Reach out with
a gentle touch and ask, "What can
I do to help you?" You will find the
inspiration comes when you take the
time to listen to nature and breathe
in your environment.

Just living is not enough...
one must have sunshine,
freedom, and a little flower.

HANS CHRISTIAN ANDERSEN

The best thing one can
do when it's raining is
to let it rain.

HENRY WADSWORTH
LONGFELLOW

Gather the flowers, but spare the buds.

ANDREW MARVELL

Community and Nature

Nature is a great teacher and offers examples of community and empathy at every turn, from gifts of each season which are freely given to the way the ecosystem supports the environment and wildlife. The soil sustains and provides new growth. The plants and shrubs become a source of nourishment to all manner of creatures, and the trees support us by providing oxygen, protection, and materials that we can use to survive. Trees also reach out to each other with a complex underground network of roots, which allows them to communicate and share nutrients with outer trees in their wood.

All of nature is interlinked and works seamlessly for the welfare of each other. We, too, are a part of this. We are born from nature, and we have an empathy with the natural world, which is instinctive, and a part of our make-up. How we relate to our surroundings and what we do to help the environment are acts of empathy. Even small things, like planting a flower or feeding the birds, have an impact and show that we care. They illustrate, without words, that we understand and appreciate the world around us and that we want to play our part.

You have first an instinct, then an opinion, then a

knowledge, as the plant has root, bud, and fruit.

RALPH WALDO EMERSON

Where you tend a rose, my lad,
A thistle cannot grow.

FRANCES HODGSON BURNETT

A HINT OF FRAGRANCE ALWAYS CLINGS
TO THE HAND THAT GIVES ROSES.

Chinese Proverb

The pedigree of honey
Does not concern the bee;
A clover, any time, to him
Is aristocracy.

Emily Dickinson

Secrets of the Seasons

AUTUMN IS A SECOND SPRING
WHEN EVERY LEAF IS A FLOWER.
Albert Camus

Kindness Warms the Heart and Soul

When you do something pleasant for someone else, or when someone does something thoughtful for you, the glow of appreciation is intangible. Kindness costs nothing to give or receive. Help someone with the garden or taking care of their outdoor space. Everyone's life around you is for the better.

**Plant
kindness
and
spread
joy**

ALL THE FLOWERS OF THE TOMORROWS
ARE IN THE SEEDS OF TODAY.

Indian Proverb

Give fools their gold, and
knaves their power; let fortune's
bubbles rise and fall; who sows
a field, or trains a flower, or
plants a tree, is more than all.

John Greenleaf Whittier

Gratitude in Action

If you have been neglecting exercise and need to get started again, remember the physical benefits of time spent in your garden. Just 20 minutes or so a day weeding, planting, and nurturing will reap great rewards—for you as well as the plants. Take time to see what is growing, how things have changed since yesterday, the shapes, colors, scents, and behavior of every small thing, from an opening flower to the buzzing circuit of a bee.

Cultivate the root;
the leaves and branches will take
care of themselves.

CONFUCIUS

Green is the prime color of the world,
and that from which its loveliness arises.

Pedro Calderon de la Barca

Nature's music
is never over;
her silences are pauses,
not conclusions.

Mary Webb

THE TREES THAT ARE SLOW TO
GROW BEAR THE BEST FRUIT.

Molière

I love nature,
I love the landscape,
because it is so sincere.
It never cheats me.
It never jests.
It is cheerfully,
musically earnest.
I lie and relie
on the earth.

Henry David Thoreau

Practice: The Earth Beneath Us

Coming directly in contact with the earth is something we don't do often as adults.

Choose a location in your garden or outdoor space that is safe and free from any detritus and take off your shoes (and socks if you are wearing them).

Stand tall, with feet parallel and hip-width apart, without locking your knees. Take your attention to the soles of your feet. Become aware of your feet in contact with the ground... the sensation of weight, the contact with the soil, grass, stones, leaves, whatever is beneath your feet.

Stand still and know you are standing.

Then lift your heels off the ground and let them fall back down, raising first one heel and then the other.

Peel your toes off the ground one by one. Next, feel your feet: the soles, the heels, the toes, the spaces under your arches.

Be aware of your feet touching the earth... this earth that is spinning beneath us, yet feels solid and stable... this earth that connects family, friends, and strangers on one continent with others on another continent...

The Earth
does not belong to us:
we belong
to the Earth.

CHIEF SEATTLE

2
Creating
a Beautiful
and Sustainable
Space

If you truly love nature, you will find beauty everywhere.

Vincent Van Gogh

Nourishing Nature Reminder

No matter where you live, spending time outdoors is one of the most precious things you can do. Even in the most built-up areas, something wonderful will be growing somewhere. Plants have a regenerative quality. They give us hope. The fact that something is growing stills the mind and relaxes the body. Plan your time so that you venture out of doors every day in your garden. Witness the beauty and create some of your own.

I GO TO NATURE
TO BE SOOTHED AND
HEALED, AND TO HAVE MY
SENSES PUT IN ORDER.

John Burroughs

The rose is fairest when't is budding new.

Sir Walter Scott

A garden to walk in and
immensity to dream in—
what more could he ask?
A few flowers at his feet and
above him the stars.

VICTOR HUGO

Any landscape is a condition of the spirit.

Henri Frederic Amiel

In all things of nature there is something of the marvelous.

ARISTOTLE

A Room with a View

What do you see when you look out your windows? What you see out of your window will feed your soul.

✿ If you have a garden or yard, love and cherish it. Expensive plants are not necessary to make it beautiful. Wild cornflowers and poppies are stunning, as are bluebells, cow parsley, and rock plants. It doesn't matter where you live, something will grow naturally.

✿ If you have no garden or yard, do you have space for a pot or two, or a window box? You can even grow herbs or vegetables. There is little as delicious as something you've grown and nurtured yourself.

✿ For inspiration, submerge yourself in the beauty of the different seasons. Take a close look at the amazing colors and textures that nature gives us.

Window
Box
Wonders

There are always flowers for
those who want to see them.

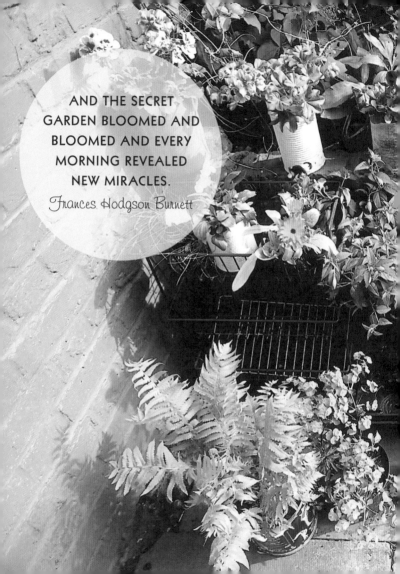

AND THE SECRET
GARDEN BLOOMED AND
BLOOMED AND EVERY
MORNING REVEALED
NEW MIRACLES.

Frances Hodgson Burnett

All gardening is landscape painting

WILLIAM KENT

Go Wild with Nature

❀ If it's possible and easy for you, designate a small square of your garden or allotment to be wild. Let the grass grow, let the wildflowers bloom, and simply watch nature take its course.

❀ If you want to encourage new growth, you could sow some wildflower seeds and sprinkle them regularly with water.

❀ Ask yourself what else you can do to help nature flourish. You might want to include a compost patch for the insects and worms or make some space for other small animals to find their home.

❀ Make a point of checking in with this space every so often and notice how it changes.

Nature
in
Motion

A good garden may have some weeds.

THOMAS FULLER

It is not the language of painters but the language of nature which one should listen to, the feeling for the things themselves, for reality is more important than the feeling for pictures.

VINCENT VAN GOGH

Make Today the Day

Learning new skills and acquiring knowledge boosts confidence and makes us happier. Discover a new plant or vegetable to add to your garden. Be curious and maybe learn about gardening with the cycles of the moon.

From plants that wake
when others sleep,
from timid jasmine buds
that keep their odor
to themselves all day,
but when the sunlight
dies away let the
delicious secret out
to every breeze that
roams about.

Thomas Moore

Act as if what you do makes a difference. It does.

William James

Grow
Your
Own
Remedies

Fractal Fascination

Fractals are structures in which the same pattern recurs at a progressively smaller scale. Think about how the vein patterns of a leaf echo the appearance of the tree itself. The geometry of fractals is all around us, including your garden—zoom in on a fern, a Queen Anne's lace flower, or a head of broccoli, and you'll find fractals. After gazing at fractals, we can appreciate the interconnected patterns of the natural world. With that appreciation can come sensations of wonder and delight, as well as quietude and tranquility.

One has to do something new
in order to see something new.

GEORG CHRISTOPH LICTENBERG

THE RICHNESS
I ACHIEVE COMES FROM
NATURE, THE SOURCE OF
MY INSPIRATION.

Claude Monet

The Funny Side of Life

Sometimes all does not go
as planned in your garden or
outdoor space. When we are
tense, we become very serious—
but turning things around in
your mind can be a great way
to change your mood and find
the lighter side of life, and often
find a solution to the situation.
Laughter and a sense of humor
are a gardener's companions and
an invitation to happiness.

Keep your face always to the sunshine, and shadows will fall behind you.

Walt Whitman

Earth laughs in flowers.

Ralph Waldo Emerson

When you go to a garden,
do you look at thorns or flowers?
Spend more time with
roses and jasmine.

Rumi

Lessons from the Garden

❀ Set yourself new challenges. Like a plant that has been pruned or newly planted, we sometimes grow more vigorously when we have been knocked back or choose to begin life anew.

❀ Respect your need for a routine. Everything in the natural world has a rhythm. It varies subtly with the seasons, but there is a pattern to each day.

❀ Take action. If you have a goal, choose to commit to it. Focus on changing the things you can and accept those things that you can't change and that are beyond your control, such as the weather.

❀ Seek guidance. If struggling with a gardening situation, reach out to other gardeners and resources.

❀ Appreciate the contrasts in your life. Notice the colors of your garden and outdoor space depending on the light and time of day.

❀ Be patient and tune into the present moment.

Don't judge each day by
the harvest you reap but
by the seeds that you plant.

Robert Louis Stevenson

Everything flows,
nothing stands still.

Heraclitus

3
Connecting
with Joy, Peace, and Calm

Plant a seed so your heart will grow.

Hafiz

Cultivate Connection

There are many ways to enrich your
connection to nature through gardening:

✿ Plant a tree in your garden

✿ Put up a bee box

✿ Feed the birds and be a bird watcher

✿ Take on an allotment in your community
garden and plant some vegetables

✿ Reduce waste and eat sustainably

Home-grown harvest and harmony

ONE TOUCH OF NATURE MAKES
THE WHOLE WORLD KIN.

William Shakespeare

Behold, my friends,
the spring is come; the earth
has gladly received the
embraces of the sun,
and we shall soon see the
results of their love!

Sitting Bull

I will focus on what I can control
and let everything else go.

Just Being

Are you someone who is always busy and on the go even with your gardening? How often do you give yourself the gift of time—the time just to pause without any agenda and simply create some space for yourself? Taking a moment and intentionally being still, allowing ourselves to be with whatever is present, is a simple practice we can do at any point, for any length of time, even in our garden. How do we do this? The easiest way is to let go of trying to do anything in particular and allow things to be exactly as they are. It's the opposite of "doing", which most of us are experts at!

There are moments when all anxiety and stated toil are becalmed in the infinite leisure and repose of nature.

Henry David Thoreau

DISCOVER THE STILLNESS OF QUIET

The power of calm

Finding a place to be still and calm is wonderfully relaxing.

Give me odorous at
sunrise a garden of
beautiful flowers where
I can walk undisturbed.

WALT WHITMAN

Release Tension

The body holds tension. Often while gardening we find ourselves in static or unusual positions with prolonged focusing and without realizing, our breathing becomes shallow and our shoulders rise. By taking deep breaths and shaking out the shoulders, you will release tension, improve your posture, and immediately feel lighter and happier.

I breathe and I know that I am

All day, free,

happy,

alone under the

heavens,

I could wander

at will through

that lovely

garden.

Victor Hugo

If we could see the miracle of a single flower clearly our whole life would change.

BUDDHA

I can make any moment a mindful moment.

The Mindful Minute

People often feel uncomfortable with the open-ended nature of meditation. With this exercise you can create a simple and time-limited meditation tailored to you that can be done in your garden at any time. Simply work out the number of breaths you normally take in a minute and use this as a guide to take a mindful minute at any time, to take a pause while gardening.

✿ Count every breath you take—breathing in and out counts as one breath. Don't worry about the number as we all breathe at different rates. This is to determine the number of breaths you take in a minute, not someone else (and it can vary hugely—in one group of 14 people, for example, it ranged from 7 to 15 breaths). If you like, you can always repeat it a couple of times to get an average.

✿ Once you have your figure simply remember it and the next time you want to practice, settle your attention on your breath and count each in- and out-breath as one up to the number you determined. That is your mindful minute.

✿ If you can do this every so often while gardening, you will be creating minutes of present-moment awareness with all the positive benefits this brings, both to you and your garden.

To nurture a
garden
is to feed
not just the body,
but the
soul.

Alfred Austin

What we plant in the soil of contemplation, we shall reap in the harvest of action.

Meister Eckhart

Home-grown gift:
a random gift of kindness

Have your visitors leave with either
a posy of flowers or the gift of some
home-grown produce from your garden,
carefully packaged. Somehow food always
tastes better, the bouquet more beautiful,
and you feel more gratitude, when it is
home-grown. Giving and receiving,
the feelings flow both ways.

Grow Gratitude

Let us be grateful to the people who make us happy, they are the charming gardeners who make our souls blossom

Marcel Proust

Peace and Vitality

Nature is an instant mood booster. It's revitalizing and it will help to restore strength and energy levels. Being in a calm and pleasant environment and connecting with the natural world improve levels of serotonin and oxytocin, hormones which make you feel good. When you are feeling low, take a mindful walk around your garden. Engage your senses as you walk, and take in not only what you can see, but what you hear, smell, feels and taste. Breathe deeply and let the power of nature and your garden infuse you with vitality.

Never does Nature say one thing and Wisdom another.

Juvenal

Every flower is a soul blossoming in nature.

GERARD DE NERVAL

Practice: Spacious Sky

Experience a connection with the earth and at the same time feel a sense of the spaciousness of the sky and the universe beyond.

Either sit, stand, or lie down in your garden or outdoor space where you have a good view of the sky. Taking a few minutes to ground yourself, feel a sense of connection to the earth through your feet, buttocks, and any other points of contact. Notice the sensations of being supported.

Turning your eyes to the sky above, open your vision to receive whatever passes across it...clouds...airplanes...vapor trails...birds... Notice if the mind is pulled away and, if so, at that moment of awareness, bring it back to the sense of connection with the ground and the spaciousness of the sky above. Open yourself up to the sky... this sky that continues unbroken across land and sea, countries, and continents... this sky that has no boundaries, that is never-ending. But also aim to maintain a sense of connection with the earth throughout.

If you look the right way, you can see that the whole world is a garden.

Frances Hodgson Burnett

Picture Credits

All photography © Ryland Peters and Small/CICO Books
unless otherwise stated.

Caroline Arber: p. 119

Simon Brown: pp. 14, 134

Jonathan Buckley: p. 108

Peter Cassidy: pp. 102, 104, 138, 38-39

Helen Cathcart: pp. 28, 135

Amanda D'Arcy: pp. 64, 94, 106, 142

Christopher Drake: pp. 75, 98

Melanie Éclare: pp. 3, 5, 18, 25, 49, 58, 60, 87, 112

James Gardiner: pp. 51, 67

Michelle Garrett: p. 39

Georgia Glynn-Smith: pp. 33, 34, 35

Catherine Gratwicke: pp. 114, 137

Caroline Hughes: pp. 10, 43, 45, 62, 63, 76, 86, 117

Kim Lightbody: p. 81

William Lingwood: p. 119

Mark Lohman: pp. 22-23

Marianne Majerus: pp. 66-67

David Merewether: pp. 15, 16, 24, 47, 78, 82, 103, 133

Emma Mitchell: pp. 19, 51, 52, 67, 85, 122

Amy Neunsinger: p. 111

Keiko Oikawa: pp. 64, 94, 106, 142

Steve Painter: p. 101

Debbie Patterson: pp. 26, 30, 59, 71, 74, 88, 126-127

Claire Richardson: pp. 120-121

Lucinda Symons: pp. 40, 55, 97

Debi Treloar: pp. 21, 31, 37, 70, 110, 129, 92-93

Pia Tryde: p. 83

Chris Tubbs: p. 44

Polly Wreford: pp. 46, 96, 100, 140

Francesca Yorke: pp. 8, 12, 57, 68, 73, 90, 91, 124, 130